Permission Slips + Praise = PR

A Chic Shepreneur's Guide To Ultimate Success

Permission Slips + Praise=PR

A Chic Shepreneur's Guide
To Ultimate Success

Published in Dallas, Georgia, by SBG Media Group and Publishing™.

ISBN 978-1-7327340-3-6

Library of Congress Control Number 2018958861

Available in electronic book also.

SBG Media Group and Publishing™

Dallas, GA

www.thescatterbrainedgenius.com/publishing

Permission Slips +

Praise =

PR

A Chic Shepreneur's Guide
To Ultimate Success

Welcome to the Permission Slips + Praise = PR journey! Ultimate success is obtained when you have a life and business that is authentically yours. (Buckle up, it only gets better from here!)

So many times, in both our professional and personal lives we have not fully unleashed how magnificent we truly are. We have often thought that we didn't want our light to outshine someone else's. In actuality, I believe that most of us can agree that we were afraid to show up. We were afraid to know what our ultimate success looked like. The fear may be different for all of us.

However, fear is fear. The acronym that I love to talk about is:

False

Evidence

Appearing

Real

This book shall help you abolish fear!

We are too powerful for the world to know who we are! It has nothing to do with popularity and it has everything to do with the significance of the work that we do and how we have to do it because if not so many people will not be as great as they could possibly be. Sister, my dear sister, it is a heavy order that we have been born into, but we must accept it. The truth of the matter is that we have no right, excuse or reason that will let us not. Even if we tried to God will not let us. It's not up to us. It's totally up to Him!

I am so excited about this book because it has allowed me to truly tap into the things that have helped me along my journey! You have seen my accolades in the beginning of this book, but I am talking about my deeper journey. The one that is all about the woman who is just Stevii. Not just the brand Just Stevii. I am more than just business cards, websites, products and services. I am a woman who is on a mission to live out God's mandate on her life. Guess what! You are too! God has given you a custom designed assignment and He has gifted you with people who are your custom designed assigned.

This book is not designed to just sit on your shelf or in the back of your trunk. This one is designed for you to learn EASY to implement tasks and tidbits that will change the trajectory of your life.

Are you ready?

Permission Slips

Remember when you were a child and you had to get that permission slip signed by your parents so that you can go on the trip. You knew that fun and freedom was on the other side of your parents signing that permission slip! You would be able to get your entire life because your friends would have their parents sign their permission slips too and you would be on bus talking and having fun. Oh, my goodness! Think back to your favorite field trip. I can remember those days vividly.

Guess what! Now we hold the power. Why? Because we hold the pen! We get to sign that phenomenal slip that opens the doors to the lives that we have only imagined. I am so blessed, excited and thankful to help you find the courage and confidence to sign the permission slip to your ideal life.

Since this book is launching on my 40th birthday October 25, 2018 I want to share 40 of the ways that I have given myself permission and I hope that you will be inspired to fill in 40 of yours as well. I left some blank space in this book for you to do so. Definitely send me your list at bit.ly/mypermissionslip

Today...

1.

I give myself permission
to know that –
what GOD has for ME
is for ME.

2.

I give myself permission

to not let worry weigh

me down.

3.

I give myself permission to turn on some music and dance.

4.

I give myself permission

to take a nap

in the middle of the day.

5.

I give myself permission to know that everything will be better than ok.

6.

I give myself permission

to try something new.

7.

I give myself permission to love with my whole heart.

8.

I give myself permission

to forgive myself

and others.

9.

I give myself permission to know how DOPE I am.

10.

I give myself permission

to be authentically me.

11.

I give myself permission to prioritize **me** over anyone else.

12.

I give myself permission

to splurge –

instead of saving.

13.

I give myself permission

to call him first

after our first date.

14.

I give myself permission

to wear that sexy dress.

15.

I give myself permission

to treat myself to

that vacation.

16.

I give myself permission

to eat dessert first.

17.

I give myself permission

to turn my dream

into reality.

18.

I give myself permission

to **not** do what is

expected.

19.

I give myself permission

to not go to the gym.

20.

I give myself permission

to embrace what feels

GREAT!

NOT Tomorrow –

Today...

21.

I give myself permission

to speak my **unfiltered**

TRUTH.

22.

I give myself permission

to show my **GENIUS**

in its totality.

23.

I give myself permission

to not know how

my biography ends.

24.

I give myself permission

to stay boldly authentic.

25.

I give myself permission

to not always do what's

nice and be naughty.

26.

I give myself permission

to sleep in.

27.

I give myself permission

to cuss and **still** be

a great Christian.

28.

I give myself permission

to act like

every day is my birthday.

29.

I give myself permission

to **not** answer

your phone call.

30.

I give myself permission

to play and not work.

31.

I give myself permission to know that I am more than enough.

32.

I give myself permission to drink champagne for no special reason.

33.

I give myself permission

to not care what **you**

think about *me*.

34.

I give myself permission

to remain unshackled.

35.

I give myself permission

to let go of my past hurts.

36.

I give myself permission to spend more time with those who love me.

37.

I give myself permission to know that fun is not a niche it's a necessity.

38.

I give myself permission

to be selfish.

39.

I give myself permission to celebrate that I don't have a ring on it yet.

40.

I give myself permission to know my biological clock is ticking and be ok.

Ok Chic Shepreneurs! I did it! Now it's your turn! I cannot wait for you to feel the freedom that giving yourself permission gives. What are you waiting to become free from? TODAY is the day to make that happen! You don't have to wait on anyone else to sign your permission slip anymore. Before you write, breathe in and breathe out. Grab you some water or wine. Whatever is your pleasure. You have permission to do whatever you want! Don't second guess what you come up with. It's truly where God is taking you to in your life and now is not the time to back down! I am thrilled to see what is happening. Don't forget to email me at

<u>bit.ly/mypermissionslip</u>

Praise

Now that we have given ourselves permission I believe that it is time for a praise party! According to Merriam-Webster's Dictionary praise is defined as to express a favorable judgment of: commend

We must praise God for Him allowing us to show up in our totality. He has blessed us immensely! We are blessed mentally, emotionally, spiritually, physically and fiscally. No, we may not have everything that we have envisioned ourselves to have but trust me, we have more than enough. We have what was promised to us. We know how we can tap into it. Since we have given ourselves permission we can dig deeper and we can begin welcoming all the rest that we desire. Isn't it amazing what can happen when we give ourselves permission for it to happen? This happens with a mindset change.

Praise is one of those things that we sometimes feel guilty about when it comes to praising ourselves. We can praise God fully because of the respect and reverence we have for Him. We can praise others fully because we value them. We praise others to the point that many times we have become Professional Clappers. What's a Professional Clapper? Its someone who does more clapping for other people but never clap for themselves and never truly allow others to clap for us. You can recognize this when someone gives you a compliment of any sort and you turn it back on them or you downplay the compliment.

Being praised can be uncomfortable if you have not seen yourself in your complete greatness. You know what, accept that you are great and accept that it's not because of anything that you did. Also, accept that you are great and that anything you did not do can diminish your greatness. You are so powerful because God has blessed you with some of His amazingness! Not having a praise party for that is like slapping God in His face. It shows that you don't appreciate what He has done for you.

This chapter on praise is important because before you can even get to the PR chapter, you must fully walk in the fact that you deserve to be praised. It is often hard to put yourself out to the level that you need to for PR to fully help you catapult to your next level of greatness. You must embrace! Embrace that you are beautiful enough, knowledgeable enough, talented enough, special enough and dynamic enough that the world needs to know you. Then praise yourself for that. Downplaying your dopeness is not sexy at all.

Elements of A Praise Party

Music! Music is a must. It does not have to be Gospel. Praise transcends genre. I believe that you can have an encounter with God listening to anything that uplifts you.

Color! I am a BRIGHT color type of Chic Shepreneur lol. I am the type who you will see with those hot pinks, fiery reds, brilliant blues and more. However, you don't have to be. Give yourself permission to wear any color that makes your spirit leap!

Fun! To have a full-fledged praise party fun has got to be part of it. Now, your fun may be different than mine and that is ok. Why? Because this is YOUR praise party. However, whenever, whatever you want to do is up to you! Yesssss! Permission slip signed!

Food! Oh, my goodness! What is a praise party without food! This one I will challenge you on to get the most opulent foods that you can find. Many times, we just let your taste buds stay tamed. This time I want you to go after the things that you have never tried before! After all this is a praise party!

These are the elements that must be at any praise party that I have. Here is some space for you to write what are must haves for yours.

PR

Permission Slips + Praise = PR

I am not a mathematician by any stretch of the imagination but the math equation that I just shared with you is one that I truly live by. It is what has allowed me to become the Author of 10 published books. It has allowed me to become a Radio Show Host, TV Show Host and Podcaster. It has allowed me to become a sought-after speaker and to create platforms not only for myself but for many other speakers to sparkle and shine on.

This signature formula is so powerful because it is the secret sauce that signature brands are made of. Many times, people don't want to tell you this. I have studied and worked in Public Relations for more than 20 years. I have watched brands of all sizes come and go. I have had PR clients, I have had my own Publicist and I have been my own Publicist. I can honestly tell you that it is not about a Press Release, an Electronic Press Kit, or any other PR element that you have ever heard about. The people who have been successful in transforming from hidden figures to becoming household names have done the work. They have left the notion of not showing how freaking awesome they are behind. They have signed their permission slips, praised themselves and never looked back. They have done it scared but they have done it. They have showed up and shown out! Those PR elements are great, but they are not everything. The truth is that when you live out your God given gift to the fullest, what I call your It Factor, your income and impact are immeasurable. No one can figure out why but you know it's because you have tapped into my favorite mathematical equation.

I hope that you are feeling the fun, freedom and flexibility that living a life of visibility and credibility affords you. It is the life that allows you to get paid for being authentically you.

Let's dive a bit deeper into what PR is. Come on in. I promise you the PR waters are fine.

One of my dear mentors once said something that broke down the walls of explaining what PR, Marketing and Advertising are.

Advertising is what you say about you. Marketing is what people say about you. PR is what you want people to say about you. I have been sharing this with my clients and they have fallen in love wiht the clarity that this brings.

Here are my Powerhouse PR Tips for Business

- Erase everything that you have ever thought about PR. Get it out of our mind. Why? Because most people are confused on what it is. PR is simply relating to the public.

- It is the ultimate know, like and trust activity. We know that people do business with those who they know, like and trust. PR helps to break down those barriers.

- PR is all about perception.

- The greatest tools that we have in 2018 for PR are livestreaming & live events.

- I specifically host live events to develop word of mouth marketing.

- As a business owner our job should be getting as many green eyes as possible on your business. Green eyes = investors

- Learn to become magnetically attractive. That is simply living out all parts of your life. This includes the good, bad, ugly and indifferent so that people can get to know you and make their decision about whether they want to become connected to you or not. Be ok with those who repel from you. They are not your ideal clients.

- Personal brands are becoming more of the norm. Pay attention to the fact that they let us into their worlds. We know so much about their lives and we love it!

- Gone are the days of the polished marketing. We want to see reality.

- Social media has become a huge game changer

- Look at how many people are discovered simply by using the power of social media

- Begin discovering podcasts that you can reach out to and get interviewed on

- Begin discovering blogs that you can guest blog on or be written about

- Get your professional headshots and speakers sheet done

- Begin livestreaming

- Begin using Eventbrite as the search engine it is for speaking engagements

- Begin writing down where you would like to show up. There is power in the pen so don't just type it out but actually write it.

- Stay open minded in regard to where you are willing to show up. Your ideal customers may just be found in some of the most unusual and unlikely places

- Always be willing to use your voice as a vessel

A Letter to

The Chic Shepreneurs

My Dearest *Chic Shepreneur,*

We have signed your permission slips, we have learned to accept praise and we have become PR Powerhouses. NOW you have started your journey! If you need additional assistance from me, know that I am here with and for you. You can always find my latest and greatest services by going to www.stevii.com/work-with-me. I am always in the mix of creating greatness for the women who God has custom designed assigned me to serve.

Love always,

Stevii

ABOUT THE AUTHOR

I am Stevii Aisha Mills.
I love God.
I rock my IT factor!
I make life fun.

Who I am...

LaTonya says – *"She is someone you need in your life! Positive, inspirational, encouraging, fun, loving, rockstar...She is all of that and more!!! You are very welcome!! Your words of inspiration and encouragement lives with me every day. I always hear your voice pushing me to live and love my life!"*

Carol – *"Where do I begin? You are my Coach, my Shero, my sister in Christ, my knowledge base, my prayer partner, my greatest influence, and most importantly, my friend! I admire your strength, beauty, wisdom and grace. May God continue to bless you with blessings on top of blessings!"*
#FavorAintFair

Nellie – *"A powerhouse in a unique package filled with love, care and concern. One who is prayerful. One who is enabled to assist in enabling you to find, learn and rock your personal it Factor like none other. And more than anything else one whose foundation is strong and centered in Christ and a family that adores her. The rest you'll find out for yourself. ...sit down watch and learn what dynamic is."*

A MESSAGE FROM THE PUBLISHER

Stevii,

It has been a few years now, four, if I am correct since we came to know of one another and since God allowed me to see a glimpse into His plan for you in the Earth – and what a plan it is!

I have watched you grow in ways that many did not have the opportunity to witness, so they don't know how much you have been hurt, the tears that you have cried, or the doubts and indecision that have been present in your mind– because you have ever so gracefully continued to show up.

As a coach – I am so proud of you. As a spiritual leader and adviser, I am grateful to God for the role He allowed me in your life and as a friend, I am excited to see you embrace 40 and continue to unfold into the woman that you are ordained to be!

Happy 40th Birthday! I know you will make the best of it!

Blessings and Love,

Miss Marilyn, aka Coach

Visit www.stevii.com

For; bookings, interviews and products